50 Science of Cooking Recipes

By: Kelly Johnson

Table of Contents

- Sous Vide Steak
- Creamy Risotto
- Perfect Poached Eggs
- Homemade Ice Cream
- Caramelized Onions
- Slow-Roasted Tomatoes
- Lemon Curd
- Molecular Gastronomy Spherification
- Chocolate Soufflé
- Butter-Cooked Lobster
- Precision Roasted Chicken
- Emulsified Vinaigrette
- Homemade Mayonnaise
- Dry-Aged Beef
- Roasted Garlic Confit
- Beurre Blanc Sauce
- Carbonara
- Frittata with Sous Vide Eggs
- Baked Alaska

- Fresh Pasta with Tomato Sauce
- Clarified Butter
- Molecular Foam
- Panna Cotta
- Chocolate Tempering
- Puff Pastry
- Classic Hollandaise Sauce
- Slow-Cooked Beef Ribs
- Poached Pears in Red Wine
- French Onion Soup
- Stock Reduction
- Smoked Salmon
- Macaron Shells
- Croissant Dough
- Sous Vide Vegetables
- Pancake Science
- Homemade Marshmallows
- Salted Caramel
- Caviar Pearls
- Cast Iron Skillet Steak
- Baking Bread with Steam

- Foam-Crafted Cocktails
- Cooked-from-Scratch Pizza Dough
- Fermented Cucumber Pickles
- Sous Vide Salmon
- Brown Butter Sauce
- Whipped Cream with Stabilizers
- Eggplant Parmigiana
- Slow-Simmered Bone Broth
- Spicy Pickled Vegetables
- Tempura Battered Shrimp

Sous Vide Steak

Ingredients:

- 1 steak (ribeye, filet mignon, sirloin, or your preferred cut)
- Salt and pepper to taste
- 2 sprigs of fresh rosemary or thyme (optional)
- 1 tbsp butter (optional)

Instructions:

1. Season the steak generously with salt and pepper.
2. Place the steak in a vacuum-seal bag or a resealable ziplock bag using the water displacement method. Add rosemary or thyme if desired.
3. Preheat your sous vide water bath to **130°F (54°C)** for medium-rare, or adjust the temperature for your preferred doneness.
4. Submerge the bagged steak into the water and cook for **1-2 hours** (up to 4 hours for extra tenderness).
5. Once done, remove the steak from the bag and pat dry with paper towels.
6. Heat a pan over medium-high heat, melt butter, and quickly sear the steak for **1-2 minutes per side** until browned.
7. Slice and serve immediately.

Creamy Risotto

Ingredients:

- 1 cup Arborio rice
- 4 cups chicken or vegetable broth (warm)
- 1/2 cup white wine (optional)
- 1/2 cup grated Parmesan cheese
- 1 tbsp butter
- 1 small onion, finely chopped
- 2 cloves garlic, minced
- Salt and pepper to taste

Instructions:

1. Heat the butter in a large pan over medium heat. Add the chopped onion and cook until softened, about **5 minutes**.
2. Add garlic and cook for **1 minute** until fragrant.
3. Stir in the Arborio rice, cooking for **2-3 minutes** until lightly toasted.
4. Pour in the white wine (if using) and stir until the liquid is mostly absorbed.
5. Add 1/2 cup of warm broth at a time, stirring constantly, and allow the liquid to be absorbed before adding more. Continue until the rice is tender and creamy, about **20-25 minutes**.
6. Stir in the grated Parmesan cheese, and season with salt and pepper to taste.
7. Serve immediately as a side dish or main course.

Perfect Poached Eggs

Ingredients:

- Fresh eggs
- Water
- 1 tbsp vinegar (optional)

Instructions:

1. Fill a saucepan with water and heat to a gentle simmer, just below boiling.
2. Add vinegar to the water if desired (it helps the egg whites stay together).
3. Crack the egg into a small bowl or ramekin.
4. Create a gentle whirlpool in the water using a spoon, then carefully slide the egg into the center of the whirlpool.
5. Poach the egg for **3-4 minutes** until the whites are set, but the yolk is still soft.
6. Use a slotted spoon to remove the egg and place it on a paper towel to drain.
7. Serve immediately, seasoned with salt and pepper.

Homemade Ice Cream

Ingredients:

- 2 cups heavy cream
- 1 cup whole milk
- 3/4 cup sugar
- 1 tbsp vanilla extract

Instructions:

1. In a mixing bowl, whisk together the cream, milk, sugar, and vanilla extract until the sugar is dissolved.
2. Pour the mixture into an ice cream maker and churn according to the manufacturer's instructions, typically for **20-30 minutes**.
3. Once churned, transfer the ice cream to a container and freeze for **2-4 hours** to firm up.
4. Serve and enjoy!

Caramelized Onions

Ingredients:

- 2 large onions, thinly sliced
- 2 tbsp butter or olive oil
- 1/2 tsp salt
- 1 tsp sugar (optional, for extra sweetness)

Instructions:

1. Heat the butter or olive oil in a large pan over medium heat.
2. Add the sliced onions and sprinkle with salt. Stir to coat the onions in the butter or oil.
3. Cook the onions slowly, stirring occasionally, for **25-30 minutes** until they are golden brown and caramelized.
4. Optional: Add sugar in the last 10 minutes of cooking for added sweetness.
5. Serve as a topping for burgers, steaks, or on sandwiches.

Slow-Roasted Tomatoes

Ingredients:

- 6–8 ripe tomatoes, halved
- 2 tbsp olive oil
- 1 tsp salt
- 1 tsp dried oregano or thyme
- 1/2 tsp garlic powder

Instructions:

1. Preheat your oven to **300°F (150°C)**.
2. Place the halved tomatoes on a baking sheet, cut side up.
3. Drizzle with olive oil and sprinkle with salt, oregano, and garlic powder.
4. Roast the tomatoes for **2-3 hours**, or until they are soft, shriveled, and slightly caramelized.
5. Serve as a side dish, on pasta, or in salads.

Lemon Curd

Ingredients:

- 1/2 cup fresh lemon juice
- Zest of 2 lemons
- 1/2 cup sugar
- 3 large egg yolks
- 1/2 cup unsalted butter, cubed

Instructions:

1. In a heatproof bowl, whisk together lemon juice, lemon zest, sugar, and egg yolks.
2. Place the bowl over a saucepan of simmering water (double boiler) and cook, stirring constantly, for **8-10 minutes** until the mixture thickens.
3. Remove from heat and stir in the cubed butter until fully melted and smooth.
4. Strain the curd through a fine mesh sieve to remove any solids.
5. Store the lemon curd in an airtight container in the fridge for up to a week.

Molecular Gastronomy Spherification

Ingredients:

- 1 cup fruit juice (or flavored liquid)
- 1 tsp sodium alginate
- 1 cup water
- 1/2 tsp calcium lactate

Instructions:

1. Blend the fruit juice with sodium alginate using an immersion blender, then let it sit for 30 minutes to remove air bubbles.
2. Mix the calcium lactate with 1 cup of water in a separate bowl.
3. Using a spoon, drop small spoonfuls of the fruit juice mixture into the calcium bath.
4. Let the spheres sit for about **2-3 minutes** to form.
5. Remove the spheres and rinse them in fresh water.
6. Serve immediately as a garnish or as part of a dish.

Chocolate Soufflé

Ingredients:

- 4 oz dark chocolate (70% cocoa)
- 1/2 cup heavy cream
- 2 tbsp butter
- 3 large eggs, separated
- 1/4 cup sugar
- 1/4 tsp cream of tartar
- Pinch of salt

Instructions:

1. Preheat your oven to **375°F (190°C)**. Butter and dust 4 ramekins with sugar.
2. Melt the chocolate with heavy cream and butter in a heatproof bowl over simmering water, stirring until smooth.
3. Whisk the egg yolks into the chocolate mixture.
4. In a separate bowl, whisk the egg whites with cream of tartar and a pinch of salt until soft peaks form. Gradually add sugar and whisk until stiff peaks form.
5. Gently fold the egg whites into the chocolate mixture.
6. Spoon the batter into the prepared ramekins, filling them about three-quarters full.
7. Bake for **12-15 minutes**, until the soufflés have risen and are set.
8. Serve immediately, dusted with powdered sugar if desired.

Butter-Cooked Lobster

Ingredients:

- 2 lobster tails, thawed if frozen
- 1/2 cup unsalted butter
- 2 cloves garlic, minced
- 1/4 cup white wine (optional)
- 1 tbsp fresh parsley, chopped
- Salt and pepper to taste
- Lemon wedges, for serving

Instructions:

1. Cut the lobster tails lengthwise down the center, and remove the meat from the shell, keeping it attached at the base.
2. Heat a large skillet over medium heat and melt the butter. Add the minced garlic and cook for **1 minute** until fragrant.
3. Place the lobster meat in the skillet and cook for **4-5 minutes per side**, spooning the butter over the lobster as it cooks.
4. Optional: Add white wine to the pan and cook for another **2 minutes**.
5. Remove from heat, season with salt, pepper, and fresh parsley.
6. Serve with lemon wedges and enjoy!

Precision Roasted Chicken

Ingredients:

- 1 whole chicken (about 4 lbs)
- 1 tbsp olive oil
- 2 tsp salt
- 1 tsp pepper
- 1 lemon, halved
- 1 bunch fresh thyme or rosemary
- 4 cloves garlic, smashed
- 2 tbsp unsalted butter

Instructions:

1. Preheat your oven to **375°F (190°C)**.
2. Rub the chicken with olive oil and season generously with salt and pepper.
3. Stuff the chicken cavity with lemon halves, garlic, and fresh herbs.
4. Place the chicken on a roasting rack inside a roasting pan and tuck the wings underneath the bird.
5. Roast for **1.5–2 hours**, basting every 30 minutes with the drippings.
6. Once done, check the internal temperature of the chicken to ensure it reaches **165°F (74°C)** at the thickest part of the thigh.
7. Rest the chicken for **10 minutes** before carving.

Emulsified Vinaigrette

Ingredients:

- 2 tbsp Dijon mustard
- 3 tbsp red wine vinegar
- 1/2 cup extra virgin olive oil
- 1 tsp honey or sugar (optional)
- Salt and pepper to taste

Instructions:

1. In a small bowl, whisk together the Dijon mustard, vinegar, and honey (if using).
2. Gradually add the olive oil while whisking vigorously to emulsify the mixture (it should thicken).
3. Season with salt and pepper to taste.
4. Serve immediately over salads, or store in an airtight container in the fridge for up to a week.

Homemade Mayonnaise

Ingredients:

- 1 large egg (at room temperature)
- 1 tbsp Dijon mustard
- 1 tbsp white vinegar or lemon juice
- 1 cup neutral oil (e.g., canola or vegetable oil)
- Salt and pepper to taste

Instructions:

1. In a food processor or blender, combine the egg, Dijon mustard, and vinegar.
2. While the processor is running, slowly drizzle in the oil, a few drops at a time at first, until the mixture starts to thicken.
3. Continue adding the oil in a slow, steady stream until fully incorporated and the mayo is thick and smooth.
4. Season with salt and pepper to taste.
5. Store in an airtight container in the fridge for up to a week.

Dry-Aged Beef

Ingredients:

- 1 large bone-in ribeye or strip steak (about 1.5–2 inches thick)
- Salt and pepper to taste
- 1 tbsp olive oil or butter

Instructions:

1. Dry-age beef in a refrigerator for **14–30 days** (or longer for a more intense flavor). You can purchase pre-dry-aged beef, or dry-age your own by placing the meat on a rack uncovered in a fridge.
2. Once aged, remove the beef from the fridge and let it come to room temperature for **30 minutes**.
3. Season the steak generously with salt and pepper.
4. Heat a skillet or grill over high heat, then sear the steak for **2-3 minutes per side** until browned.
5. Finish cooking to your desired doneness using indirect heat or by roasting in the oven at **400°F (200°C)** for **5–10 minutes**.
6. Rest the steak for **5 minutes** before slicing and serving.

Roasted Garlic Confit

Ingredients:

- 1 head garlic, cloves peeled
- 1 cup olive oil (enough to cover the garlic)
- 2 sprigs fresh thyme (optional)
- 1 bay leaf (optional)

Instructions:

1. Preheat your oven to **250°F (120°C)**.
2. Place the garlic cloves in an oven-safe dish, and pour the olive oil over the garlic until it's fully submerged.
3. Add thyme and bay leaf if using.
4. Roast for **45 minutes to 1 hour**, until the garlic is soft, golden, and fragrant.
5. Remove from the oven and let cool.
6. Store the garlic and oil in an airtight container in the fridge for up to **2 weeks**.

Beurre Blanc Sauce

Ingredients:

- 1/2 cup dry white wine
- 1/4 cup white wine vinegar
- 1/4 cup shallots, finely chopped
- 1 cup unsalted butter, cubed and cold
- Salt and pepper to taste

Instructions:

1. In a saucepan, combine the wine, vinegar, and shallots.
2. Bring to a boil and reduce the liquid by about **half**.
3. Reduce heat to low and whisk in the cold butter cubes, one at a time, until fully incorporated and the sauce thickens.
4. Season with salt and pepper to taste.
5. Serve immediately over fish, chicken, or vegetables.

Carbonara

Ingredients:

- 12 oz spaghetti or pasta of choice
- 4 oz pancetta or guanciale, diced
- 3 large eggs
- 1/2 cup grated Pecorino Romano cheese
- 1/4 cup grated Parmesan cheese
- Salt and freshly ground black pepper to taste

Instructions:

1. Cook the pasta in salted water according to the package instructions until al dente.
2. While the pasta cooks, heat a pan over medium heat and cook the pancetta or guanciale until crispy, about **5 minutes**.
3. In a mixing bowl, whisk together the eggs, Pecorino Romano, Parmesan, salt, and pepper.
4. Once the pasta is cooked, reserve 1 cup of pasta water and drain the rest.
5. Add the hot pasta to the pan with the crispy pancetta, tossing to coat.
6. Pour the egg and cheese mixture over the pasta, tossing quickly to create a creamy sauce.
7. Add reserved pasta water, a little at a time, until the sauce reaches the desired consistency.
8. Serve immediately, topped with additional cheese and black pepper.

Frittata with Sous Vide Eggs

Ingredients:

- 6 large eggs (cooked sous vide at **167°F (75°C)** for **45 minutes**)
- 1/2 cup milk or cream
- 1 cup vegetables (spinach, bell peppers, mushrooms, etc.), cooked and chopped
- 1/2 cup shredded cheese (cheddar, mozzarella, or your choice)
- 1 tbsp olive oil or butter
- Salt and pepper to taste

Instructions:

1. Preheat your oven to **375°F (190°C)**.
2. Whisk the sous vide-cooked eggs with milk or cream, and season with salt and pepper.
3. Heat olive oil or butter in an ovenproof skillet over medium heat.
4. Add the cooked vegetables and sauté for **2-3 minutes**.
5. Pour the egg mixture over the vegetables in the skillet and cook for **3-4 minutes** without stirring.
6. Sprinkle cheese on top and transfer the skillet to the oven.
7. Bake for **10-12 minutes** until the frittata is set and golden on top.
8. Serve immediately, sliced into wedges.

Baked Alaska

Ingredients:

- 1 sponge cake (store-bought or homemade)
- 4 cups vanilla ice cream
- 4 large egg whites
- 1/4 tsp cream of tartar
- 1/2 cup sugar
- 1 tsp vanilla extract

Instructions:

1. Preheat your oven to **500°F (260°C)**.
2. Place the sponge cake on a baking sheet.
3. Soften the ice cream slightly and spread it over the cake to form a thick layer. Freeze the cake with the ice cream for at least **1 hour**.
4. In a bowl, beat the egg whites with cream of tartar until soft peaks form. Gradually add sugar, continuing to beat until stiff peaks form.
5. Remove the cake from the freezer and cover it with a thick layer of meringue.
6. Bake in the oven for **3-5 minutes**, or until the meringue is golden brown.
7. Serve immediately.

Fresh Pasta with Tomato Sauce

Ingredients for Pasta:

- 2 cups all-purpose flour
- 2 large eggs
- 1 tbsp olive oil
- 1/2 tsp salt

Ingredients for Tomato Sauce:

- 1 can (28 oz) crushed tomatoes
- 2 tbsp olive oil
- 1 garlic clove, minced
- 1 tsp dried basil
- 1 tsp dried oregano
- Salt and pepper to taste

Instructions:

1. To make the pasta, mound the flour on a clean surface and make a well in the center. Add the eggs, olive oil, and salt into the well.

2. Gradually mix the flour into the eggs until a dough forms. Knead for about **10 minutes** until smooth and elastic.

3. Roll out the dough thinly using a pasta machine or rolling pin, then cut it into your desired pasta shape (fettuccine, tagliatelle, etc.).

4. Bring a pot of salted water to a boil and cook the pasta for **2-3 minutes** until al dente. Drain and set aside.

5. For the sauce, heat olive oil in a pan and sauté the garlic for **1 minute**. Add the crushed tomatoes, basil, oregano, salt, and pepper. Simmer for **15 minutes**.

6. Serve the pasta with the tomato sauce.

Clarified Butter

Ingredients:

- 1 lb unsalted butter

Instructions:

1. Melt the butter in a saucepan over low heat.

2. Once melted, allow it to simmer for **5-10 minutes**. The milk solids will separate and float to the top.

3. Skim off the milk solids with a spoon, then carefully pour the clear yellow butterfat into a separate container, leaving the solids behind.

4. Store in an airtight container for up to **2 weeks** in the fridge.

Molecular Foam

Ingredients:

- 1 cup liquid (fruit juice, broth, etc.)
- 1 tsp lecithin powder

Instructions:

1. In a bowl, mix the liquid with lecithin powder.
2. Use an immersion blender to blend the mixture for **30-60 seconds** until foam forms.
3. Spoon the foam over your dish and serve immediately.

Panna Cotta

Ingredients:

- 2 cups heavy cream
- 1/2 cup whole milk
- 1/4 cup sugar
- 1 tsp vanilla extract
- 1 packet (about 2 1/4 tsp) gelatin
- 3 tbsp cold water

Instructions:

1. In a small bowl, bloom the gelatin by sprinkling it over cold water. Let it sit for **5 minutes**.
2. In a saucepan, heat the heavy cream, milk, and sugar over medium heat until it just begins to simmer. Stir to dissolve the sugar.
3. Remove from heat and add the bloomed gelatin, stirring until fully dissolved.
4. Stir in the vanilla extract.
5. Pour the mixture into individual ramekins and refrigerate for at least **4 hours** until set.
6. Serve with fresh berries or a berry compote.

Chocolate Tempering

Ingredients:

- 8 oz high-quality chocolate (dark, milk, or white)

Instructions:

1. Chop the chocolate into small, even pieces.

2. Melt **2/3 of the chocolate** in a heatproof bowl over simmering water or in the microwave in short bursts, stirring every 30 seconds.

3. Once melted, remove from heat and add the remaining **1/3 of the chocolate**, stirring until fully melted and smooth.

4. Test the temper by dipping a spoon into the chocolate; it should harden quickly and be glossy.

5. Use the tempered chocolate for dipping, molding, or coating.

Puff Pastry

Ingredients:

- 2 1/2 cups all-purpose flour
- 1 tsp salt
- 1 cup cold unsalted butter, cubed
- 1/2 cup cold water

Instructions:

1. In a food processor, pulse the flour and salt. Add the butter and pulse until the mixture resembles coarse crumbs.
2. Gradually add the cold water and pulse until the dough starts to form.
3. Turn the dough out onto a floured surface and knead briefly to bring it together.
4. Roll out the dough into a rectangle, fold it into thirds, and refrigerate for **30 minutes**.
5. Repeat the rolling and folding process **3-4 times**, refrigerating between folds.
6. Use the puff pastry for your favorite baked goods.

Classic Hollandaise Sauce

Ingredients:

- 3 large egg yolks
- 1 tbsp lemon juice
- 1/2 cup unsalted butter, melted
- Salt and pepper to taste

Instructions:

1. In a heatproof bowl, whisk together the egg yolks and lemon juice.
2. Place the bowl over a saucepan of simmering water (double boiler method). Whisk constantly until the yolks begin to thicken.
3. Gradually whisk in the melted butter, a little at a time, until the sauce is thick and smooth.
4. Season with salt and pepper to taste.
5. Serve immediately with eggs Benedict or other dishes.

Slow-Cooked Beef Ribs

Ingredients:

- 4 beef ribs
- 1/4 cup olive oil
- 1 tbsp garlic powder
- 1 tbsp onion powder
- 1 tbsp smoked paprika
- 1/2 cup beef broth
- Salt and pepper to taste

Instructions:

1. Preheat your oven to **300°F (150°C)**.
2. Rub the beef ribs with olive oil, garlic powder, onion powder, smoked paprika, salt, and pepper.
3. Place the ribs in a roasting pan and pour the beef broth around them.
4. Cover with aluminum foil and slow-cook for **3-4 hours** until the meat is tender and easily pulls away from the bone.
5. Remove from the oven, discard the foil, and serve.

Poached Pears in Red Wine

Ingredients:

- 4 pears, peeled and cored
- 1 bottle red wine (750 ml)
- 1/2 cup sugar
- 2 cinnamon sticks
- 2 cloves
- 1 orange, sliced
- 1 tsp vanilla extract

Instructions:

1. In a saucepan, combine the red wine, sugar, cinnamon sticks, cloves, orange slices, and vanilla extract.
2. Bring the mixture to a simmer over medium heat, stirring until the sugar dissolves.
3. Add the pears to the saucepan and cook gently for **25-30 minutes**, turning occasionally, until tender.
4. Remove the pears and reduce the wine mixture to a syrup over medium heat for about **10-15 minutes**.
5. Serve the pears with the reduced sauce poured over the top.

French Onion Soup

Ingredients:

- 4 large onions, thinly sliced
- 4 tbsp butter
- 1 tbsp olive oil
- 4 cups beef broth
- 1 cup dry white wine
- 2 sprigs fresh thyme
- 2 bay leaves
- 1 baguette, sliced
- 1 1/2 cups Gruyère cheese, shredded
- Salt and pepper to taste

Instructions:

1. In a large pot, melt butter and olive oil over medium heat. Add the onions and cook, stirring frequently, for **30-40 minutes** until the onions are caramelized.
2. Add the white wine and cook for **5 minutes** to deglaze the pot.
3. Add the beef broth, thyme, and bay leaves. Bring to a simmer and cook for **30 minutes**.
4. Season with salt and pepper to taste.
5. Preheat the broiler. Ladle the soup into oven-safe bowls, top with a slice of baguette, and sprinkle with Gruyère cheese.
6. Place under the broiler for **2-3 minutes** until the cheese is melted and golden.
7. Serve hot.

Stock Reduction

Ingredients:

- 4 cups stock (chicken, beef, or vegetable)
- 1 tbsp olive oil
- 1 tbsp butter (optional)

Instructions:

1. Pour the stock into a saucepan over medium heat.
2. Bring it to a gentle simmer and reduce the liquid by **half**, which should take about **20-30 minutes**.
3. Stir occasionally to prevent burning.
4. If desired, add butter at the end for a richer flavor and texture.
5. Use the reduced stock in sauces, soups, or gravies.

Smoked Salmon

Ingredients:

- 1 lb salmon fillets, skin on
- 1/4 cup kosher salt
- 1/4 cup sugar
- 1 tbsp black peppercorns, crushed
- 1 tbsp fresh dill, chopped
- Wood chips for smoking (e.g., alder, hickory)

Instructions:

1. Mix the salt, sugar, peppercorns, and dill in a bowl.
2. Rub the mixture generously on the salmon fillets and wrap them in plastic wrap.
3. Refrigerate for **4-6 hours** or overnight.
4. Rinse off the curing mixture and pat the salmon dry.
5. Prepare your smoker by heating the wood chips and placing them in the smoker.
6. Smoke the salmon at **180°F (82°C)** for **1-2 hours**, depending on the thickness of the fish, until the desired level of smokiness is achieved.
7. Serve chilled or at room temperature.

Macaron Shells

Ingredients:

- 1 cup powdered sugar
- 1 cup almond flour
- 3 large egg whites
- 1/4 cup granulated sugar
- 1/2 tsp vanilla extract

Instructions:

1. Sift the powdered sugar and almond flour together to remove any lumps.
2. In a clean, dry bowl, whip the egg whites with an electric mixer until foamy. Gradually add the granulated sugar and beat until stiff peaks form.
3. Gently fold the dry ingredients into the meringue in batches until fully incorporated.
4. Transfer the batter to a piping bag and pipe small circles onto a parchment-lined baking sheet.
5. Tap the baking sheet on the counter to remove air bubbles, then let the shells sit at room temperature for **30 minutes** until a skin forms.
6. Preheat the oven to **300°F (150°C)** and bake the shells for **15-20 minutes**.
7. Let them cool completely before filling with your desired filling.

Croissant Dough

Ingredients:

- 4 cups all-purpose flour
- 1/4 cup sugar
- 2 tsp salt
- 1 tbsp active dry yeast
- 1 1/4 cups cold water
- 3 tbsp unsalted butter, melted
- 1 1/4 cups unsalted butter, cold

Instructions:

1. In a large bowl, mix flour, sugar, salt, and yeast. Add cold water and melted butter, then knead until a dough forms.
2. Cover the dough and let it rest for **1 hour** to rise.
3. Roll the dough out into a rectangle. Place the cold butter in the center and fold the dough around it.
4. Roll the dough into a long rectangle and fold it into thirds. Repeat this process **3 times**, refrigerating the dough for **30 minutes** between folds.
5. After the final fold, roll the dough out, cut it into triangles, and shape into croissants.
6. Let the croissants rise for **1 hour**, then bake at **375°F (190°C)** for **15-20 minutes** until golden and flaky.

Sous Vide Vegetables

Ingredients:

- 4 cups mixed vegetables (carrots, zucchini, bell peppers, etc.)
- 2 tbsp olive oil
- Salt and pepper to taste

Instructions:

1. Preheat your sous vide water bath to **185°F (85°C)**.
2. Cut the vegetables into uniform pieces and place them in a vacuum-seal bag with olive oil, salt, and pepper.
3. Seal the bag and place it in the water bath. Cook for **30-45 minutes** until tender.
4. Remove the vegetables from the bag and serve immediately, or sear them in a hot pan for extra flavor.

Pancake Science

Ingredients:

- 1 cup all-purpose flour
- 1 tbsp sugar
- 1 tsp baking powder
- 1/2 tsp baking soda
- 1/2 tsp salt
- 3/4 cup buttermilk
- 1 large egg
- 2 tbsp melted butter

Instructions:

1. In a bowl, whisk together the dry ingredients.
2. In another bowl, whisk the wet ingredients together.
3. Combine the wet and dry ingredients, stirring until just mixed (don't overmix).
4. Heat a griddle or skillet over medium heat and grease lightly.
5. Pour batter onto the skillet and cook for **2-3 minutes** on each side, until golden brown.
6. Serve with syrup, butter, or toppings of choice.

Homemade Marshmallows

Ingredients:

- 1/2 cup cold water
- 3 packets unflavored gelatin
- 1 cup sugar
- 1/2 cup corn syrup
- 1/2 tsp vanilla extract
- Powdered sugar for dusting

Instructions:

1. In a small bowl, sprinkle the gelatin over cold water and let it bloom for **5 minutes**.
2. In a saucepan, combine sugar, corn syrup, and 1/2 cup water. Bring to a boil, stirring until sugar dissolves.
3. Remove from heat and add the bloomed gelatin. Stir until dissolved.
4. Transfer the mixture to a stand mixer and beat on high for about **10 minutes** until fluffy and stiff peaks form.
5. Add vanilla extract and beat for another minute.
6. Pour the marshmallow mixture into a greased pan and let it set for **4-6 hours**.
7. Dust with powdered sugar and cut into squares.

Salted Caramel

Ingredients:

- 1 cup sugar
- 6 tbsp unsalted butter, cut into pieces
- 1/2 cup heavy cream
- 1 tsp vanilla extract
- 1 tsp sea salt

Instructions:

1. In a medium saucepan, melt the sugar over medium heat, stirring constantly. The sugar will clump before it melts, so keep stirring until it's completely liquefied and turns a golden amber color.
2. Once melted, add the butter and stir until it's fully incorporated.
3. Carefully add the heavy cream (it may bubble up), and continue to stir until smooth.
4. Remove from heat and stir in vanilla extract and sea salt.
5. Let the caramel cool before using. Store in an airtight container.

Caviar Pearls

Ingredients:

- 1/4 cup fruit juice (e.g., pomegranate, blueberry, etc.)
- 1/4 tsp agar-agar powder
- 1/4 cup olive oil (or another neutral oil)
- 1/4 tsp calcium chloride (optional, for more firmness)

Instructions:

1. In a saucepan, heat the fruit juice and agar-agar over medium heat. Bring it to a boil, stirring constantly. Once it starts boiling, reduce the heat and simmer for **2-3 minutes** until the agar-agar is dissolved.
2. In a separate bowl, mix the calcium chloride with a little water (if using).
3. Pour the olive oil into a shallow dish or container. Place it in the fridge to chill.
4. Drop the agar-agar mixture into the chilled oil, using a spoon or dropper. The mixture will form into small pearls as it hits the cold oil.
5. After the pearls form, remove them from the oil and rinse them with water.
6. Serve the caviar pearls as a garnish for dishes like salads, sushi, or desserts.

Cast Iron Skillet Steak

Ingredients:

- 2 steaks (ribeye, sirloin, or your preferred cut)
- 2 tbsp olive oil
- 2 tbsp unsalted butter
- 2 garlic cloves, smashed
- 2 sprigs fresh thyme or rosemary
- Salt and pepper to taste

Instructions:

1. Let the steaks come to room temperature, about **30 minutes** before cooking.
2. Preheat a cast iron skillet over medium-high heat.
3. Pat the steaks dry and season them generously with salt and pepper.
4. Add olive oil to the skillet, and once it's hot, place the steaks in the pan. Sear for **3-4 minutes** on each side, or until a golden-brown crust forms.
5. Add the butter, garlic, and herbs to the skillet. Once the butter melts, spoon it over the steaks to baste.
6. Continue cooking for an additional **2-4 minutes** per side, depending on your desired doneness.
7. Remove the steaks and let them rest for **5-10 minutes** before serving.

Baking Bread with Steam

Ingredients:

- 3 cups all-purpose flour
- 1 1/2 tsp salt
- 1 tsp active dry yeast
- 1 cup warm water
- 1 tbsp olive oil
- 1 tbsp sugar

Instructions:

1. In a bowl, combine the warm water, sugar, and yeast. Stir and let sit for **5-10 minutes** until frothy.
2. Add the flour and salt to the yeast mixture. Stir until a dough forms, then knead for **8-10 minutes** until smooth.
3. Cover the dough with a damp cloth and let it rise for **1-2 hours** until doubled in size.
4. Preheat the oven to **450°F (230°C)**. Place a shallow pan with water on the bottom rack to create steam.
5. Punch down the dough, shape it into a loaf, and place it on a baking sheet or in a Dutch oven.
6. Score the top of the dough and bake for **25-30 minutes**, or until golden brown and hollow-sounding when tapped on the bottom.
7. Let the bread cool before slicing.

Foam-Crafted Cocktails

Ingredients:

- 2 oz spirit (vodka, gin, rum, etc.)
- 1 oz simple syrup
- 1 oz fresh citrus juice (lemon, lime, etc.)
- 1 egg white (or aquafaba for a vegan version)
- Ice
- Garnish of choice (herbs, fruit, or spices)

Instructions:

1. Add the spirit, simple syrup, citrus juice, and egg white (or aquafaba) into a shaker.
2. Dry shake (shake without ice) vigorously for **15-20 seconds** to create foam.
3. Add ice to the shaker and shake again for **15-20 seconds** to chill the mixture.
4. Strain into a glass and garnish with a sprig of rosemary, a lemon twist, or any garnish of choice.
5. Serve immediately.

Cooked-from-Scratch Pizza Dough

Ingredients:

- 2 1/4 tsp active dry yeast
- 1 1/2 cups warm water
- 3 1/2 cups all-purpose flour
- 2 tbsp olive oil
- 1 tsp sugar
- 1 tsp salt

Instructions:

1. In a bowl, combine the warm water, sugar, and yeast. Stir and let sit for **5-10 minutes** until frothy.

2. Add the flour, salt, and olive oil to the yeast mixture. Stir to combine, then knead the dough for **8-10 minutes** until smooth and elastic.

3. Place the dough in an oiled bowl, cover it with a damp cloth, and let it rise for **1-1.5 hours** until doubled in size.

4. Punch the dough down and divide it into portions. Roll each portion into a pizza shape and top with your favorite toppings.

5. Preheat the oven to **475°F (245°C)**. Bake the pizza for **12-15 minutes**, or until the crust is golden and the cheese is bubbly.

Fermented Cucumber Pickles

Ingredients:

- 4-5 small cucumbers, sliced
- 2 cups water
- 2 tbsp sea salt
- 2 cloves garlic, smashed
- 1 tbsp mustard seeds
- 1 tbsp peppercorns
- 2-3 sprigs fresh dill
- 1 bay leaf (optional)

Instructions:

1. In a pot, heat the water and sea salt, stirring to dissolve the salt. Let it cool to room temperature.
2. Place the cucumbers, garlic, mustard seeds, peppercorns, dill, and bay leaf in a clean jar.
3. Pour the cooled saltwater over the cucumbers until fully submerged.
4. Cover the jar loosely with a lid or cloth and leave it at room temperature for **3-7 days**, checking daily for fermentation.
5. Once the pickles are tangy enough, store them in the fridge.

Sous Vide Salmon

Ingredients:

- 2 salmon fillets
- 1 tbsp olive oil or butter
- Salt and pepper, to taste
- 1 sprig fresh dill (optional)
- 1 slice lemon (optional)

Instructions:

1. Preheat your sous vide machine to **125°F (52°C)**.
2. Season the salmon fillets with salt and pepper.
3. Place each fillet in a vacuum-seal bag with a drizzle of olive oil or butter, and optionally add a sprig of dill and a slice of lemon.
4. Seal the bags and submerge them in the water bath. Cook for **45 minutes**.
5. Once done, remove the salmon from the bag and sear briefly in a hot pan for **30 seconds to 1 minute** on each side if you prefer a crispy skin.

Brown Butter Sauce

Ingredients:

- 1/2 cup unsalted butter
- 1 clove garlic, minced
- 1 tbsp fresh sage or thyme (optional)
- Salt and pepper, to taste

Instructions:

1. In a pan, melt the butter over medium heat.
2. Once melted, continue to cook, stirring constantly, until the butter begins to foam and turns a golden-brown color.
3. Add the garlic and herbs (if using) and cook for **1-2 minutes** until fragrant.
4. Season with salt and pepper to taste, and drizzle over pasta, vegetables, or meat dishes.

Whipped Cream with Stabilizers

Ingredients:

- 1 cup heavy whipping cream
- 1 tbsp powdered sugar
- 1/2 tsp vanilla extract
- 1/2 tsp unflavored gelatin (optional, for extra stability)

Instructions:

1. If using gelatin, dissolve it in **1 tbsp of warm water** and let it bloom for **5 minutes**.
2. In a mixing bowl, combine the heavy cream, powdered sugar, and vanilla extract.
3. Whisk until soft peaks form, and if using gelatin, add it once the cream is slightly thickened. Continue whipping until stiff peaks form.
4. Serve immediately, or store in the fridge for a few hours.

Eggplant Parmigiana

Ingredients:

- 2 eggplants, sliced into 1/2-inch rounds
- 2 cups marinara sauce
- 1 1/2 cups shredded mozzarella cheese
- 1/2 cup grated Parmesan cheese
- 2 eggs, beaten
- 1 cup breadcrumbs
- 1/2 cup all-purpose flour
- Olive oil for frying
- Salt and pepper, to taste

Instructions:

1. Preheat the oven to **375°F (190°C)**.
2. Season the eggplant slices with salt and let them sit for **15-20 minutes** to draw out moisture, then pat dry.
3. Set up a breading station with flour, beaten eggs, and breadcrumbs. Dip each eggplant slice first into the flour, then the egg, and finally the breadcrumbs.
4. Heat olive oil in a pan over medium-high heat. Fry the breaded eggplant slices until golden brown on each side, about **2-3 minutes per side**.
5. In a baking dish, layer the fried eggplant slices with marinara sauce, mozzarella, and Parmesan.
6. Bake for **20-25 minutes** or until the cheese is melted and bubbly.

Slow-Simmered Bone Broth

Ingredients:

- 2-3 lbs beef, chicken, or pork bones
- 2 carrots, chopped
- 2 celery stalks, chopped
- 1 onion, halved
- 3 cloves garlic, smashed
- 2 tbsp apple cider vinegar
- Water to cover
- Salt and pepper, to taste
- Fresh herbs (rosemary, thyme, bay leaves, etc.)

Instructions:

1. Preheat the oven to **400°F (200°C)**. Roast the bones in a baking pan for **30-45 minutes** until browned.
2. Transfer the bones to a large pot or slow cooker. Add the vegetables, garlic, vinegar, and herbs.
3. Cover with water and bring to a boil. Reduce the heat and let it simmer gently for **12-24 hours**.
4. Skim off any impurities that rise to the surface.
5. After simmering, strain the broth and discard the solids.
6. Season with salt and pepper to taste. Store in the fridge or freeze.

Spicy Pickled Vegetables

Ingredients:

- 1 cucumber, sliced
- 1 carrot, sliced
- 1/2 small cauliflower, broken into florets
- 1/2 cup white vinegar
- 1/2 cup water
- 1 tbsp salt
- 1 tbsp sugar
- 2 cloves garlic, smashed
- 1 tbsp mustard seeds
- 1 tsp red pepper flakes
- 1 tsp black peppercorns

Instructions:

1. Place the vegetables in a jar or container.
2. In a saucepan, combine the vinegar, water, salt, and sugar. Bring to a boil, then remove from heat.
3. Add the garlic, mustard seeds, red pepper flakes, and peppercorns to the jar with the vegetables.
4. Pour the hot brine over the vegetables, ensuring they are fully submerged.
5. Let cool, then refrigerate for **3-7 days** before enjoying.

Tempura Battered Shrimp

Ingredients:

- 1 lb shrimp, peeled and deveined
- 1 cup all-purpose flour
- 1/2 cup cornstarch
- 1/2 tsp baking powder
- 1 cup ice-cold water
- Salt, to taste
- Vegetable oil for frying

Instructions:

1. Heat the oil in a deep fryer or large pot to **350°F (175°C)**.
2. In a bowl, mix the flour, cornstarch, baking powder, and a pinch of salt.
3. Add the ice-cold water and stir to combine. The batter should be lumpy for the best texture.
4. Dip the shrimp into the batter, allowing any excess to drip off.
5. Fry the shrimp in the hot oil until golden and crispy, about **2-3 minutes**.
6. Remove from oil and drain on paper towels. Serve with a dipping sauce.